# What Is Citizenship?

by Jennifer Boothroyd

first step nonfiction

Lerner Publications ◆ Minneapolis

**LERNER**

**SOURCE**

Expand learning beyond the printed book. Download free, complementary educational resources for this book from our website, www.lerneresource.com.

The images in this book are used with the permission of: © Szefei/Dreamstime.com, p. 4; © Blend Images/KidStock/Getty Images, p. 5; © Hero Images/Getty Images, p. 6; © John Moore/Getty Images, p. 7; © iStockphoto.com/Justin Horrocks, p. 8; © Scott Olson/Getty Images, p. 9; © iStockphoto.com/ fstop123, pp. 10, 15, 18; US Air Force photo by Master Sgt. Patrick J. Cashin, p. 11; © Blend Images-Hill Street Studios/Getty Images, p. 12; © Steve Skjold/Alamy, p. 13; © iStockphoto.com/theboone, p. 14; © iStockphoto.com/rappensuncle, p. 16; © iStockphoto.com/ebstock, p. 17; © Todd Strand/ Independent Picture Service, p. 19; © iStockphoto.com/DougLloyd, p. 20; US Navy photo by Mass Communication Specialist 1st Class Collin Turner, p. 21; © iStockphoto.com/asiseeit, p. 22.

Cover: © Gabe Souza/Portland Press Herald via Getty Images.

Main body text set in ITC Avant Garde Gothic Std Medium 21/25.
Typeface provided by Adobe Systems.

Lerner Publications Company
A division of Lerner Publishing Group, Inc.
241 First Avenue North
Minneapolis, MN 55401 USA

For reading levels and more information, look up this title at www.lernerbooks.com.

Library of Congress Cataloging-in-Publication Data

The Cataloging-in-Publication Data for *What Is Citizenship?* is on file at the Library of Congress.
ISBN 978-1-4677-8575-4 (lib. bdg.)
ISBN 978-1-4677-8623-2 (pbk.)
ISBN 978-1-4677-8624-9 (EB pdf)

Manufactured in the United States of America
1 – CG – 7/15/15

# Table of Contents

# Who Are Citizens?

Look at this brand-new **citizen**!

A person born in a country
is a citizen.

**Immigrants** are people who move to another country.

Immigrants must pass a test to become US citizens.

They can become citizens in their new country.

# Citizen Rights

In the United States, citizens have many **rights**.

Citizens can disagree with their leaders.

They can share their ideas in public.

They can choose their own
religion.

The military protects the country.

They are protected.

They help choose leaders.

They should be treated fairly.

US citizens have many **responsibilities**.

Voting Today

Voting A-K

They vote.

They follow the laws.

This person is working to get a law changed.

They suggest ways to make laws better for everyone.

Taxes pay for things such as parks and schools.

They pay **taxes**.

They help others.

The bald eagle is a symbol of the United States.

They respect their country's symbols.

They may serve in the
**military**.

How can you be a good citizen?

# Glossary

**citizen** –  a person who lives in a country and has rights in that country

**immigrants** – people who move to a new country

**military** – the army, the navy, the marines, and the air force

**responsibilities** – jobs you do to help others in your group

**rights** – freedoms that should be guaranteed

**taxes** – money collected by the government to pay for services

# Index